Facets of the Soul

Hannah Moore

Presentation by *BookLeaf Publishing*

Web: www.bookleafpub.com

E-mail: info@bookleafpub.com

ISBN: 978-93-95784-02-3

First edition 2022

DEDICATION

Honestly, I dedicate this book to myself.

For all the times I chose therapy over the destructive and pathetic person I could have been.

For little Hannah, it's safe to come out now.

For the healing still to come.

ACKNOWLEDGEMENT

Let's keep this brief.
I want to acknowledge my husband. For seeing me as someone worth loving. For holding open a safe space for healing and growing within our marriage. For feeding me encouragement and consistency. I appreciate you, husband.

And I'd like to acknowledge my good friends Amanda and Jess. For letting me verbally process the shit out of everything from childhood trauma and the latest fight my husband and I have had, to whether Tim Tams are just big KitKats and what you would do if you were a man for the day. You guys have kept me just the right amount of insane.

Husband

I like it when
Our feet or bums touch in bed
You kiss my forehead

I know you love me when
You do a double squeeze
You prepare me bread, meat and cheese

I roll my eyes when
You forget to wear your wedding ring
You try and do a Ben Ching

We know what we mean when
We say "I love YouTube. Or U2…THE BAND"
Or "Is that David's Master Plan?"

You make me laugh when
We fight over putting the sunshield up in the car
I'm not wearing one and you say "oh, my
favourite bra"

Other cute things include
Postman Pat, a Grace-cup-of-tea,
Helicopter ponytail, the way you look at me.

Date Night

Six years and six months
Sweet, considerate husband
My perfect date night

An introverts dream
Staying in, not going out!
Such a thoughtful plan

Relax, wash your hair
We'll have bread, cheese, meats to eat
A quiet, slow night

Snuggle on the couch
Share with me your emotions
I'll mirror them back

To finish the night
Let's snuggle up and keep warm
Camping in the car

Perth

The sun winked at me through a tunnel,
She blinked at me through the trees.
She eased atop the ocean,
And teased me along with the breeze.

The sun called me out underneath her,
To stand tall and be warmed by her gaze.
She whispered of hope and restoration,
And kissed me on my tilted-back face.

The Night

The sun drifts beneath the horizon. You awaken.
You fill the world, blanket everything you can
reach. Rush into every space.
Marvel at each soul. Envelop them into your
care.
Mind the babes tucked into tight sheets, words
of love pressed to their brows. Soothe them
softly.
Watch over the street, the fork in the road, the
endless dwellings. Part for those who pass
through.
Peer from the edges of the light, listen to the
babble of voices, laughter, music, that emerge as
a door is thrown open. Wrap those musicians,
dancers, lovers into your shadows.
Observe that shy kiss, that lingering farewell,
those first strains of love. Caress their
blush-stained cheeks.
Eavesdrop on the late talkers, who form their
dreams and heartaches into words. Gather those
spilled words, keep them safe.
Discover the secret silhouette, feet wet in the
grass, eyes turned up at the moon. Let the stars
shine for them.

Notice the blaring noises, the forgotten
murmurs, televisions working late. Observe
through forgotten windows, cracks in curtains.
Tease the hushed one sitting in the soft glow,
reading late. Entice them to you.
Hear the whispers, skin shifting, soft sighs.
Drape yourself over their unhesitating embrace.
Pursue the silent thief, his bountiful retreat.
Cover his crimes until the morning.
Conceal the animals that prowl, that see right
through you. You cannot protect their prey.
Survey the still forms sleeping, gentle snores,
deep breathing. Consider their dormant
dreaming.
Pass beside the ones who walk early, who see
your beauty, who don't hide from you. Quiet the
world for them.
Outrun the chalky light that insists at your edges.
Burn away, smudges of colour on fire.
Say goodbye. Disappear for the sunlight hours.
Only your shadows will remain, a reminder.
What wonders wait for the night.

An Account

When I get to heaven,
And turn toward the throne,
Will I be anxious?
Will I walk on my own?

Or will Jesus walk beside me?
Will he look me in the eye?
Will I be full of confidence?
Will I be fearful, will I cry?

Does it matter what I've been through?
Does it matter what I've done?
Or is all that really matters,
That I gave my heart to the Son?

Will God be wrathful toward me,
And Jesus step in to defend?
Will I fall apart at his presence?
There will be no room to pretend.

How can I ask God to save me,
When I won't be able to lie?
When I know he sees all of me,
When we both know I deserve to die.

Maybe I'm worried,
that when I arrive,
Jesus will be busy.
And I won't survive.

Powerless

I heard a man say,
"I've been fortunate to never feel powerless".
And the tide of my soul rushed out so quickly
I thought everyone would hear the scream,
the emptying, the sudden vacuum.

Because I cannot count the times.

My agency was silenced, my body was abused.
My spirit was diminished, my love was misused.

I was conditioned to be helpless; I wasn't
allowed a voice.
My words, my body, my truth, I wasn't given a
choice.

Sometimes even now I still struggle to say
something when I should,
There's a whisper inside me saying, "don't
embarrass them; be good!"

As if it's my responsibility to make sure they
don't get upset,
I have to remind myself it was to a child they
posed a threat.

My redemption story hasn't been storming the
world and never backing down,
It has been about settling into myself and
learning not to get overwhelmed.

A quiet re-teaching of everything I know,
I can speak! I can laugh, I can grieve. I can
grow.

Favourite four letter words

Late
Shit
Stay
Naps
Warm
Play

Open
Feel
Lick
Wish
Love
Dick

Rest
Sock
Chat
Fuck
Lane
Wrap

Lord
Kiss
Walk
Eyes
Food
Talk

Mate
Cold
Pray
Hand
Dogs
Okay

Salt
Read
Blue
Jars
Star
Grew

Forgiveness

For years
I clung to my trauma
Holding it within me
A shield

These too big, too raw
Too hard to forgive
Wounds of a child
Brought into adulthood

I fought to learn
To let go
But my hands were claws
And they felt justified

Surely God wouldn't ask
Not this impossible task
Undeserving act
Not of me

But He did
As an act of obedience
As He forgives me
Undeservingly

I can choose
Forgiveness
To accept what He did for me
To trust and obey

Chaotic Confession

I'm scared of the dark,
And being unable to outswim a shark.

I can't reverse a trailer,
Or bear the thought of failure.

I always worry about what people think,
I hate that when I'm embarrassed my whole face
turns pink.

I don't want to be a mother,
I wish I never had a brother.

I never used to like my red hair,
I've never liked the taste of beer.

I feel anxious going new places,
I don't like being stuck in small spaces.

I believed I wasn't worthwhile,
I see red when I'm told to "smile!"

Friendship

You accepted me before I learnt how to.
You listened as I processed.
You held a space open for my story to dwell within.
You encouraged me in so many different and important ways.
You loved me!
You never judged me.
You made time for me.
You were always honest with me.
You prayed for me.
You made me laugh at our ridiculous antics and topics of conversation; so varied and vast!
You did all these things and it helped me realise that I matter.
You have been a pivotal part of my restoration.
Because although physically I cried very few tears, you caught my pain, turned it into rain, and used it to water me and help me grow.

Lies I Once BeLIEved

Nobody likes you,
You don't matter,
You're not important,
You aren't worthy.

You let everyone down,
You're not good enough,
Everyone is better than you,
You're too broken for love.

People who love me will reject me,
My opinion doesn't matter,
Conflict always hurts,
It's dangerous to be wrong.

Love is only for perfect people,
Appearances are more important than the truth,
I should hide who I am,
Boys can break the law and still be more loved
than girls.

Companion

The companion is a familiar aching pressure.
They wrap my brow in an unrelenting band, my
temples in a vice.
They take purchase inside my head while I grow
and hope and dream.
Though they fight to steal the brightest parts of
the day, they are restricted to their border of
pain.
Love and laughter bubble through the rest of me.

Companion, you can dull my edges, you can
pierce my thoughts, but you cannot block out the
sun.
Life is mine.

Marriage Is Hard

People say that marriage is hard, but they don't tell you how.

They don't tell you that you argue in different ways, that communicating gets harder, that you don't just "get" each other; you must work on it.

They don't tell you that you'll trigger each other, that the way he brushes aside what you say will make you feel small and like your voice doesn't matter.

They don't tell you that he won't understand your emotions, so he won't listen, he'll just try to fix things, so you won't feel heard or cared about.

They don't tell you that you will feel attacked every time he questions anything you've done, and so you will attack him back.

They don't tell you that because you had to parent yourself for so long, you'll resent having to do anything that even looks like taking care of him; why can't he do it himself?!

They don't tell you that you might drift apart, but you'll never drift together, you must do work on that part.

They don't tell you that couples counselling will be the best thing you'll ever do for your marriage, learning to care for your marriage, to

communicate in a healthy way, listen to each
other, and make each other feel loved in the
ways that you need.
They don't tell you that as you start caring for
each other and looking for ways to make each
other feel special, your love for the other grows
more tender.
They don't tell you that you can hold each other
and create a safe healing space where you can
make your marriage even stronger.
They don't tell you that marriage can be
beautiful if you work through the hard parts.
They probably do tell you that it's worth it
though.
And it is.

February 22

The earth growls and rolls beneath,
When the seams of the house creak,
The panic and fear creep in.

What is moving beneath the earth's pregnant
belly?
A shudder runs down the earths back, a ripple
across her skin.
The anxiety grips you.

The roaring begins, your world moving, jolting,
shaking.
Glass breaking, your belongings thrown around,
your house ripping apart,
Time to get out.

There is water pouring out somewhere next to
you, there is smoke and dust.
There is plaster and glass and debris on the
stairs,
You run down in your bare feet.

The front door is stuck, a door handle rips off in
your hand.

Out the back door and into dust so thick you
can't see anything.
No cell signal.

You climb your way out of the backyard, into
this new city,
Tears streaming down your face, what will you
do?
You are only eighteen.

The world is on pause, until suddenly it isn't,
People are running past, cars jammed into
intersections, traffic lights a suggestion.
So much noise.

Cars stop as people embrace, everyone is crying,
Police, fire trucks, ambulances scream through
space where there wasn't room before,
Lives colliding.

You stand in shock at your day's violent
interruption,
While everything else is in fast-forward,
Your life is at a stand-still.

When I First Fell in Love (2012)

I love him.
This smile he does, so wicked and laughing at
the same time.
The unintentional pouty look whenever he looks
in the mirror.
The puppy-eyes when he's trying to be cute.
The way he looks at me.
The way he tucks me under his arm when we're
walking.
Or finds my hand to hold.
When he reaches across to hold my hand when
he's driving.
His eyes.
When he pulls me across the bed to spoon.
Cuddling with him.
Feeling his body on top of mine, the weight of it.
His beard and the love-rug.
His smiley round cheeks.
Feeling his hands on me.
That he likes the blue and white jelly-beans.
And the berry skittles.

I love most everything about him.

Hypocrisy

Psychologically healing
Angry she wouldn't do the same
Ignoring my spiritual healing
When I'll only ever be healed in His name.

This miracle always seemed too hard
Because I couldn't see past my own works
I couldn't see how she would ever learn
My words had only ever seemed to make things
worse.

While I was raging about her stubborn nature
God was transforming her thinking
When she opened up to me,
Her confession had me blinking.

I had accused her of not wanting to heal
But I had been the stubborn one
I tried to do it on my own
And had never once included the Son.

Now it's time for my confession
Something I really should have known
Why didn't I believe that God could do,
Something I couldn't manage on my own?

Now I Know

I didn't know
How many times I would second-guess my
choice.
The guilt I would feel at choosing myself.

I didn't know
How many conversations I would play out in my
head,
What I would say to you and what had already
been said.

I didn't know
How many times I would wonder how you are,
How you are doing now.

I didn't know
That losing our friendship would be a relief.
That sometimes I would wish it had cost me
even less.

I didn't know
I would fear running into you.
I wouldn't care what you had told our old mutual
friends.

I didn't know
That it would cost me another friendship.
That I would eventually stop being angry at you.

I didn't know
If I could bear to watch you destroy your life,
And mine at the same time.

I didn't know
How hard it would be to choose me,
But I would do it again.

Now I know,
Making the choice is only the first part,
Allowing yourself the space to feel the grief is
the rest.

Blessings and Brokenness

I've accepted that I will never be finished
healing.
The fissures of brokenness run too deep in some
places.
There is no undoing or forgetting some wounds.

But I won't stop learning on this journey.
Already I learnt how to have empathy for
myself.
And a confidence I never thought I would
possess.

The way I can read other people comes from the
trauma.
And it is often a blessing.
A way to open connection between two souls.

Being highly sensitive to my environment can be
tiring.
The information I always hold.
But it helps me find my place in the world.

My self-awareness and introspection keep me
honest.
I can't lie to myself.

It lets me process my thoughts, feelings and
experiences.

I'm so grateful for the therapy I've had.
Each teaching me something for specific
seasons.
Slowly preparing me for who I will be.

I will continue to grow bit by bit.
Soothing my tempestuous inner child.
Allowing her to heal and slowly flourish.

Hold my hand, little one.
See how far we've come.
We learnt to love ourself.

www.ingramcontent.com/pod-product-compliance
Lightning Source LLC
Chambersburg PA
CBHW061323140726
47998CB00007B/2524